the offical guide to
JAZZ
Dancing

the offical guide to JAZZ Dancing

Allen Dow
with Mike Michaelson

 CHARTWELL BOOKS INC.

Book design and production: MacDonald Graphics
Photography: Patrick K. Snook
Type composition: Hagle
Production coordinator: Ruth Guest

THE OFFICIAL GUIDE TO BALLROOM DANCING
Copyright © 1980 Quality Books, Inc.
Published by Chartwell Books Inc.
A Division of Book Sales Inc.
110 Enterprise Avenue
Secaucus, New Jersey 07094

1 2 3 4 5 6 7 8 9 10

Manufactured in the United States of America

Library of Congress Cataloging in Publication Data

Dow, Allen, 1931–
    The official guide to jazz dancing.

    Includes index.
    1. Jazz Dance.   I. Michaelson, Mike, 1934– joint
author.   II. Title
GV1753.D65   793.3   79–55238
ISBN 0–89009–334–2

contents

introduction

Of all forms of dance, jazz dancing is the most difficult to define. It is an elusive hybrid. It borrows readily from classical ballet, from modern dance, from tap dancing, boogie-woogie, rock and even disco. Even its name defies labeling, because traditional jazz music is the heart and soul of improvization.

Jazz, says Webster, is: "American music characterized by improvization, syncopated rhythms, contrapuntal ensemble playing, and special melodic features peculiar to the individual interpretation of the player." One story, perhaps apocryphal, has it that the term originated from a honky-tonk piano player improvizing at the keyboard who, when asked to identify the soul-stirring music he was playing, said, "Man, I'm jus' jazzin' around."

Just as jazz music is the quintessence of individual interpretation, so jazz dance is a vehicle for individual and highly stylized improvization by the jazz teacher, dancer or choreographer. Yet, jazz dance is not without structure and discipline. It is a vibrant art form that can be as demanding of technical perfection and style as ballet. Despite its freedom for interpretation, jazz dance has many constants—positions, movements and techniques which, over the years, have developed into an integral part of the jazz dancer's repertoire.

Positions for arms and feet, for example, have been adapted from classical ballet and incorporated into jazz—but with much license to adapt these positions to suit the choreography. Isolation of individual parts of the body, such as head, shoulders and knees, are used to provide dramatic media of expression. "Jazz hands," with fingers expressively splayed, also has become a standard in the jazz dancer's lexicon, as are the strong, driving "jazz walk" and the "jazz run," performed with the back foot dragging and the arms working in counter-motion. Then there is the dramatic stag leap, as well as jazz adaptations of such ballet techniques as the relevé, the plié and the chassé. Together, all of these elements—and many more—provide the choreographer and the dancer with a repertoire of movement that lends itself to an infinite variety of music.

Unlike a chic new dance fad that explodes into the public eye for a frenetic,

6

short-lived burst of popularity and then slips into obscurity or settles into a small niche in the over-all dance scene, jazz—which is a theatrical rather than a social dance—has proved itself to be durable. It is a dance form that adapts, improvizes and changes with the times. It is as comfortable with disco as it was with ragtime. It also has become a universal form of dance expression, lending itself to the stage, to film and to television. And it is becoming increasingly popular throughout the world.

Jazz traces its roots to Africa through the folk dances of the slaves in the Deep South. Its earliest practitioners were black, many of whom danced in the streets, collecting coins tossed by passers-by. A direct predecessor of today's jazz dance was the Cake Walk, popularized by slaves who would compete in high-stepping dance contests, the prize for which often would consist of a cake.

Soon came the early minstrel shows and, in 1921, the musical, *Shuffle Along* opened on Broadway, the vanguard of a decade of popular all-black musicals. Dances such as the Black Bottom, the Charleston, the Jersey Bounce and the Rooster Strut began to enjoy epic popularity. Jazz-dance exponents included such colorful performers as Williams and Walker, King Rastus Brown, and John W. Bubbles. Latterday jazz-dance greats include such performer-choreographers as Bob Fosse, Gus Giordano, Tony Stevens and Peter Gennaro.

As dancing moves into the decade of the 1980s, movies such as *All That Jazz* and stage shows such as *Chorus Line* give yet another exciting new dimension to the ever-changing face of jazz.

stretch exercises

Jazz dancing, which borrows heavily from ballet, can be just as strenuous and as physically demanding as that classical form of dance. Regular exercising and warm-up periods are important, both as a safeguard against injury and as a means of improving movement and technique. In fact, many of the stretch and isolation exercises included in this and the following chapter are an integral part of the jazz dance. Even after years of dance experience. professional dancers and teachers continue to work regularly at these all-important exercises.

This chapter deals with stretch exercises. These are essential to stretch out the muscles to permit the full extension used in jazz-dance movements and also to minimize the risk of injury with painful torn or pulled muscles. However, if you are a beginner, you should approach these exercises prudently. Learn to walk before you run. Until your body becomes supple and acquires the level of conditioning that regular exercising and dance practice surely will bring, be sure not to push your body beyond its limits. Work up gradually to the full number of repetitions recommended for each exercise; do not force full extension until your body has become limber enough to achieve it.

Beginners also should not be overly concerned about getting into positions according to the assigned counts. This will come with practice. For example, it may, in the beginning, take from four-to-eight counts, instead of the prescribed two counts, to reach the required positions. A good example is the demanding Inverted Split and Fold exercise. It calls for raising the legs and hips in two counts, a maneuver which may take the novice up to eight counts to execute. That's okay, too.

Some of the following exercises are done at center floor—either at the studio or in your home; others are done at the ballet bar. In most cases, a table or chair may be substituted for the ballet bar. However, for bar exercises that utilize a pulling technique, be sure to use a stable prop.

If you work regularly and conscientiously on the exercises in this and the following chapter, you not only will improve your dance movements and technique, but you also will get yourself in fine physical shape.

SUPINE POSITION BATTEMENT EXERCISES

These exercises should begin in supine position, head and back flat on floor, legs extended, arms relaxed on floor at sides of body. To achieve effective stretching for hamstrings and muscles at backs of legs, it is important to keep the legs straight (knees do *not* bend).

Exercise 1

COUNT 1
Kick up right leg with arched foot (as to do a battement).

COUNT 2
Flex foot, curling toes toward body.

COUNT 3
Arch foot, as in count 1.

COUNT 4
Lower right leg to floor.

Repeat this sequence with left leg. Do at least four 8-count sets. Then:

Come to sit-up position, stretching arms and upper torso toward feet in a pulsing (bouncing) motion—pulsing for eight counts.

This total exercise also may be done with legs open in "V" position.

Exercise 2

COUNTS 1-2
Kick up right leg with arched foot (pointed toe).

COUNTS 3-4
Right leg crosses to left side of body, hands grasp leg between ankle and knee (as close as possible to foot), arms pull straight leg toward head in pulsing fashion (for approximately 8 counts).

COUNTS 5-12
Hold position for eight counts.

COUNTS 13-14
Return to supine position, right leg up, as in counts 1-2.

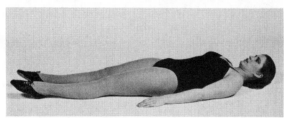

COUNTS 15-16
Lower right leg to floor.

As before, the exercise should be repeated with the other leg. Repeat the total sequence three or more times.

Exercise 3

COUNT 1
Kick up right leg with arched foot.

COUNT 2
Grasp ankle with both hands and pull leg toward head in a pulsing fashion while remaining flat on back (approximately eight pulses). After pulsing, release leg and lower to floor to two counts.

Repeat with the other leg. Repeat the total sequence three or more times.

INVERTED SPLIT AND FOLD EXERCISE

Begin in supine position, as previously described.

COUNTS 1-2
Raise both legs on count 1, raise hips (with hands on hips) on count 2, using one flowing motion into shorter stand position. Legs should be pointed straight up with arched feet.

COUNTS 3-4
Legs open in split position, count 3; hold, count 4.

COUNTS 5-6
Return to shoulder stand position (with legs and feet together with hand on hips), count 5; hold, count 6.

COUNTS 7-8
Right leg forward, toward head (with arched foot), left leg back (straddle split), count 7; hold, count 8.

COUNTS 9-10
Legs return to together position, as in counts 5-6.

COUNTS 11-12
Left leg forward toward head (with arched foot), right leg back (straddle split), count 11; hold, count 12.

COUNTS 13-14
Legs return to together position.

COUNTS 15-16
Legs begin to move over head toward floor, back begins to roll inward.

Counts 15-16-17-18 are done in one flowing movement.

COUNTS 17-18
Feet reach floor and legs and feet begin to stretch away from head, as back and neck begin to roll, arms extended on floor away from body. Hold this position for approximately 8 counts.

COUNTS 19-20
Legs return to upright position as in counts 5-6.

stretch exercises : 17

COUNTS 21-22
Legs open in split position, count 21; hold, count 22.

COUNTS 23-24
Legs return to together position.

COUNTS 25-26
Legs begin to go over head.

COUNTS 27-28
Arms extended to floor at approximately 45° angle away from body, back begins to roll to floor.

COUNTS 29-30-31-32
Back continues to roll toward floor, ending with back, legs and heels on floor (in supine position) at count 32.

Note: When legs are in upright position, feet together (as in counts 5-6), ankle exercises may be added by alternately flexing and pointing the feet. Also, split position may, if desired, be sustained for longer periods. Rolled position (as in counts 17-18) also may be sustained. Dismount with straight legs—do *not* bend knees.

SITTING TWIST EXERCISE

This twisting exercise, done in which often is referred to as a "swastika position," is executed by twisting two-to-four counts in one direction, and then reversing the twist, two-to-four counts in the opposite direction.

Begin with left leg in front, with knee bent, and right leg in back, with knee bent, arms extended. Twist upper torso to left, head turning left, 2-to-4 counts.

Reverse twisting motion from left to right, head turning right.

Note: This sequence should be repeated for a total of at least 4 times. Sequence then should be reversed, with right leg in front, left leg in back.

SITTING TWIST WITH PUSH-UP

COUNTS 1-2
Sitting in "swastika position," right leg in front, left leg in back, twist upper torso and head to left.

COUNTS 3-4
Reverse twist, upper torso and head twisting to right.

COUNTS 5-6
While torso is twisted to right, do push-up, hands to floor and pressing body toward floor (elbows bent).

COUNTS 7-8
Arms straighten, raising body off floor.

Repeat sequence for a total of at least 4 times and then reverse by putting left leg in front, right leg in back and execute 4 repetitions.

JAZZ SPLIT AND STRETCH EXERCISE

COUNTS 1-to-8
Extend right leg to front (leg straight), left leg in back (knee bent, as in "swastika"), both arms extended toward right foot and upper torso pulling toward right foot in pulsing fashion.

COUNTS 1-to-8
Left arm raises and reaches over head, head turning to left (look upward), giving side stretch.

Sequence should be repeated a total of 2-to-4 times and then reversed by putting left leg in front, right leg back.

HIP AND THIGH STRETCH EXERCISE

METHOD 1
Sit in upright position with back straight, bottoms of feet together, feet pulled close to body. Knees pulse toward floor, 4-8 counts; then hold pressure, knees pulling toward floor, 4-8 counts. (You may find it helpful to use elbows to push knees down.) Repeat sequence 4-8 times.

METHOD 2
Identical to Method 1, except pulsing is assisted by hands pushing down on knees.

LEG RAISE EXERCISE

METHOD 1
From yoga position, take right foot with right hand, hand on bottom of foot (reaching from inside, not outside, of leg), thumb toward body. Then extend leg (with foot flexed) upward and outward, pulling with right hand. Then return to yoga position. Use 2 counts to raise leg, 2 counts to come down.

Exercise should be repeated for a total of 4-8 times and then reversed (with opposite leg and arm).

METHOD 2
Leg raise exercise also may be done with arched (pointed) feet. Arching the foot usually will allow more extension than the flex. However, the flex gives more stretch to backs of legs.

RIB CAGE EXTENSION EXERCISE (With Sit-Up and Stretch)

Begin in supine position with arms and hands on floor alongside body.

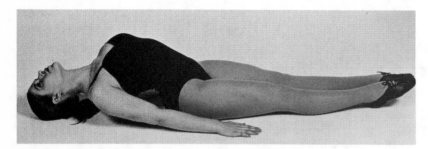

COUNTS 1-2
Expand rib cage as to lift chest toward ceiling (back lifts off floor). Important: Do not put weight on top of head to achieve this position.

COUNT 3
Continue to lift rib cage, causing upper torso to lift off floor as to do a sit up (however, note that head hangs back). If necessary, you may use hands as support.

COUNT 4
Continue to raise body into sitting position, head remaining back.

COUNTS 5-6
Reach upper torso toward feet, pulsing counts 5-6-7-8 and continuing for a total of 7 counts. Then begin to return to supine position, counts 5-6-7-8.
    Total sequence should be repeated about 4 times.

FORWARD SPLIT

Begin in standing position, legs apart and to side of body, palms of hands to floor. Legs slide apart to sides into split position. Note: Hands and arms are used to support body to prevent over-split. Hands and arms should be relatively close to body to keep majority of weight on legs rather than on arms. Try to hold this position for 8-16 counts. To come out of split, let weight fall back as to sit, or bend legs, bringing them back to original position.

SIDE SPLIT

From standing position, move right leg forward, left leg back, upper torso facing forward (right) leg. As body lowers to floor, palms of hands go to floor, right hand on right side of body, left hand on left side of body. As in the previous exercise, hands and arms are used to support weight. This is important for beginners, who usually will not be able to obtain full extension. Try to hold split position for 8-16 counts. Then reverse, left leg in front, right leg back, so as to provide equal stretch.

SITTING SIDE STRETCH

Sit with legs in wide "V." Left arm reaches over head and toward right foot, head facing forward or slightly upward, right arm in front of body reaching toward left leg. Note: Do not lean forward in this exercise. Pulse 4-8 counts, then reverse. Total sequence should be repeated 2-4 times.

SITTING FORWARD STRETCH

COUNT 1
Sit in upright position, legs extended in a wide "V," hands on hips.

COUNT 2
Bend upper torso forward, arms and head extended forward.

COUNT 3
Return to beginning position.

COUNT 4
Extend arms upward in "V."

COUNT 5
Turn upper torso to right, hands placed on each side of forward leg.

COUNT 6
Extend upper torso and arms toward right leg.

COUNT 7
Raise upper torso and arms.

COUNT 8
Turn upper torso forward, arms still extended upward.

Total sequence should be reversed and repeated a total of 4-8 times.

THE RACK

Begin sitting, right leg extended forward, left leg back (as in swastika position), arms extended upward.

Important: If you have any problems with your knees, this exercise should not be attempted.

COUNTS 1-8
Extend upper torso and arms toward right leg, pulsing 8 counts.

COUNTS 1-2
Return to sitting position.

COUNTS 3-8
Lie back during these counts, remaining in this position for approximately 8 counts.

This sequence should be reversed, with left leg forward, right leg back.

STRETCH AND ROLL EXERCISE

Begin in supine position.

COUNTS 1-2
Extend right leg upward and pull leg toward head with hands on lower leg.

COUNTS 3-4
Pull right leg toward left side and down to floor, continuing to stretch leg toward head, body beginning to roll over. Note: At this point, front of left leg and instep of left foot is on floor.

COUNTS 5-6-7-8
Body continues to roll, left arm extends forward, left leg bends at knee, pulling left foot pointing toward head. Continue to stretch right leg toward head with right arm. Hold this position, continuing to stretch for an additional eight counts (9-16), then reverse (counts 1-8) and repeat with opposite leg and side.

STRETCHING EXERCISES AT THE BALLET BAR

LEG AND SIDE STRETCH EXERCISE

Place right leg on bar and slide right leg and body to right, causing stretch. Left hand on bar for support, right arm and upper torso stretching toward right foot with 8 pulsing counts.

Right arm stretching in rounded motion over head, body leaning to left side with 8 pulsing counts. Note placement of left hand on bar, left arm crossing body. This total exercise should be repeated at least two times and then reversed using other leg.

LEG AND BACK STRETCH EXERCISE

Right leg on bar, stretching to right with 8 pulsing counts as in previous exercise.

Turn body left, holding bar with right hand, front of right leg and instep of foot on bar. Grasp left ankle with left hand, stretch head and back toward left foot in 8 pulsing counts.

Reverse this exercise, using opposite leg and opposite side of body.

BATTEMENT STRETCH

Begin standing parallel to bar with left hand on bar, weight on left foot (left knee bent), right foot approximately 12 inches behind left on ball of right foot. Hips remain over supporting (left) leg as right heel presses to floor, stretching back of right leg; then raise and lower right heel in pulsing motion to 8 counts.

COUNT 1
Lift right leg forward and up toward head in kicking motion with pointed (arched) foot—both legs straight for this motion. (Extension of leg may be greater or less than illustrated, according to the individual's flexibility, which should increase with practice.)

COUNT 2
Return to original position, right foot back, on ball of foot.

COUNTS 3-8
Execute heel press in pulsing motion

Note: This press and battement exercise will be repeated in more detail in chapter on positions and technique.

Battement stretch also may be done to side and back without heel presses, kicking counts 1, returning counts 2 (approximately 8 counts each). Side battement stretch may be done parallel to bar or with back to bar, holding bar with both hands (as illustrated).

This, as all stretches, should be reversed and done with other side of body with other leg.

DÉVELOPPÉ STRETCH

Begin standing parallel to bar with left hand on bar, weight on both feet.

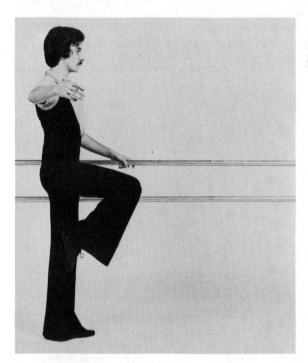

COUNTS 1-2
Raise right knee in front of body, right foot to left knee, weight on left foot.

COUNTS 3-4
While right knee remains elevated, extend lower part of leg with foot arched.

COUNTS 5-6
Return to position used in counts 1-2

COUNTS 7-8
Right foot returns to floor to original standing position.

This stretch may be done to side and back in same fashion and to same counts, except raised knee would turn out to side (right knee to right side), counts 1-2.

Repeat this exercise for 2-4 sets, then reverse, putting right hand on bar facing opposite direction and using other leg.

LEG LIFT

Begin standing parallel to bar, right hand on bar.

COUNTS 1-2
Raise left leg with knee bent, left arm inside of leg. Grasp left heel with left hand, palm toward heel, thumb toward back side of heel.

COUNTS 3-4
Extend left leg by lifting with left hand.

COUNTS 5-6-7-8
After holding for 4 counts at stretch position, return to position used for counts 1-2. Then repeat by extending leg (counts 3-4), holding counts 5-6-7-8.

This extension exercise should be repeated approximately 4 times and then reversed, using other hand on bar, facing opposite direction, and using other leg.

RELEVÉ ARCH

Begin standing close to bar, back to bar, with both hands holding bar (note: hands should reach over *top* of bar).

COUNTS 1-2
Come to relevé position (high on bottoms of toes) with legs straight.

This exercise is performed at the ballet bar (as demonstrated by Mark) or by holding onto a suitable piece of furniture. Kim is used in this series of pictures to present a side view of the arch.

COUNTS 3-4
Stretch away from bar with strong arch, head hanging back, legs remaining straight.

COUNTS 5-6
Return to position of counts 1-2.

COUNTS 7-8
Drop heels to floor as knees bend into demi-plié. This exercise should be repeated approximately eight times.

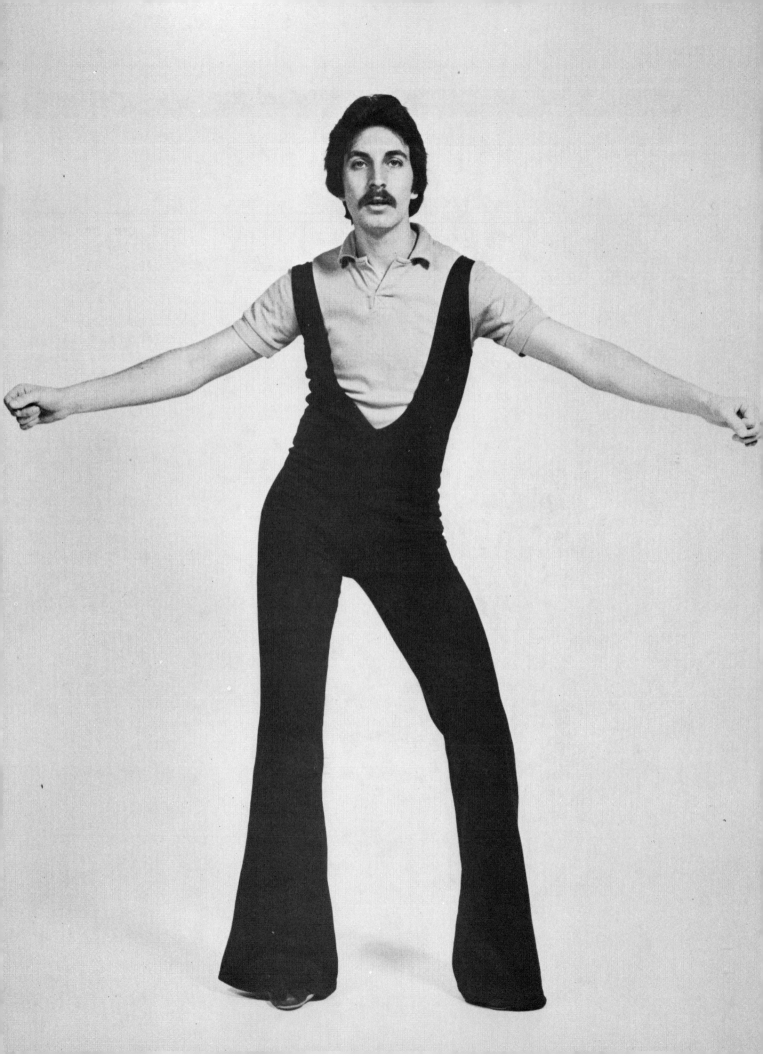

isolation exercises

In jazz dancing, the technique of isolation is a highly stylized form of expression. It involves moving only certain parts of the body and not others—such as the isolated movement of the head or shoulders or rib cage. The exercises in this chapter will help the dance student develop this ability to control the movement of various parts of the body, one at a time. They also will assist in developing strength, agility and that essential ingredient of graceful performance, coordination.

As with the stretch exercises provided in the previous chapter, isolation exercises should be an integral part of a pre-dance warm-up session. They should be done after you have performed a series of muscle-limbering stretch exercises.

When these isolation techniques have been mastered, they can be choreographed into individual dance routines. As you become more adept at these isolations, you will be able to use them in combinations. For example, the isolation of the shoulders may be coordinated with isolation of the rib cage.

HEAD ISOLATION (Forward and Back)

Begin with hands on hips, feet in jazz second (legs comfortably apart).

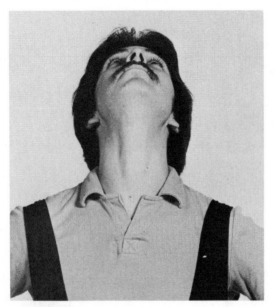

COUNT 1
Head back.

COUNT 2
Head returns to upright position.

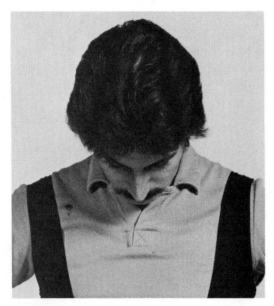

COUNT 3
Head forward, chin tucked in.

COUNT 4
Head returns to upright position, as in count 2.

This sequence should be repeated about 4 times, then done without stopping in upright position, as, head back, count one; head forward, count 2. This non-stop motion is done for about 8 counts.

HEAD ISOLATION (Side-to-Side)

Begin as in previous exercise.

COUNT 1
Head side left.

COUNT 2
Head returns to upright position.

COUNT 3.
Head side right.

COUNT 4
Head returns to upright position.

This isolation may be done by passing through the upright position instead of pausing. Beginners are advised to use this pause to avoid pulling neck muscles.

Repeat this sequence 4 times, then use 8 counts for the non-stop motion.

HEAD ISOLATION (Profile)

Begin as in two previous exercises.

COUNT 1
Turn head to left, as to look over left shoulder.

COUNT 2
Return head to face forward, beginning position.

COUNT 3
Turn head to right, as to look over right shoulder

COUNT 4
Return to beginning position.

Repeat sequence 4 times, then use 8 counts for non-stop motion (omitting forward position)—head moving continuously from left to right.

HEAD ROLL ISOLATION

Begin as in preceding head isolation exercises.

COUNT 1
Tilt head to left.

COUNT 2
Begin to roll head forward, tucking in chin.

COUNT 3
Head continues to roll from forward position to right side.

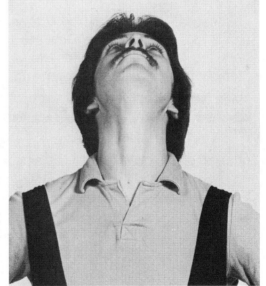

COUNT 4
Head continues to roll from side to back.

As you become more adept at this exercise, the motion should develop into a fluid, continuous roll and, instead of using 4 counts, the complete head roll may be done in two, or even one, count.

This exercise should be repeated at least 4 times and then reversed, starting with head to right side and rolling clockwise.

SHOULDER ISOLATION

Begin standing upright, feet in jazz second (as in head isolation exercises), arms extended out to sides (second position).

Begin standing upright, feet in jazz second as in head isolation exercises), arms extended out to sides (second position).

COUNT 1
Raise right shoulder (not arm).

COUNT 2
Right shoulder forward.

COUNT 3
Right shoulder down.

COUNT 4
Right shoulder back.

This sequence should be done at least two times, then done 4 more times in a continuous rolling motion (eliminating pauses). Exercise then should be done with opposite (left) shoulder. After exercising both shoulders in this fashion, exercise then should be reversed (shoulder up, back, down, forward).

OPPOSITION SHOULDERS

Begin in upright position, feet in jazz second. Arms may be extended to second position or placed with hands on hips or placed at sides. Beginners may find hands on hip the easiest position. Isolations also may be done with arms down, as illustrated, or in any other position.

This exercise should be done in a rolling, fluid motion.

COUNT 1
Raise both shoulders

COUNT 2
Right shoulder forward, left shoulder back, both shoulders down.

COUNT 1
Raise both shoulders.

COUNT 2
Right shoulder back, left shoulder forward, both shoulders down.

RIB CAGE ISOLATION (Side Stretch)

Begin in upright position, feet in second for balance, as in head isolations. For beginners, this exercise may be more effectively done with hands on hips.

COUNT 1
Rib cage (upper torso only) pulls left.

COUNT 2
Return to upright position

COUNT 3
Rib cage pulls right

COUNT 4
Return to upright position

Rib cage motion also should be done in side-to-side fashion without pausing in upright position.

Because beginners may have a tendency to move their hips while learning this isolation exercise, it often is easier to begin practicing it while sitting upright on a chair (back *not* touching back of chair). Additionally, when doing this exercise while seated, it may aid the beginner to put hands on upper leg, fingers facing inward (toward inner thighs). While pulling rib cage right, push right hand against right leg; while pulling rib cage left, push left hand against left leg. To become more aware of this isolation as you are performing it, you will find it helpful to look into a mirror.

RIB CAGE EXPANSION AND CONTRACTION

Begin in same position as for previous rib cage isolation exercise.

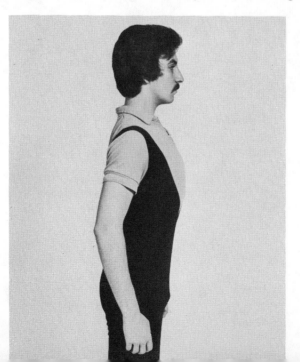

COUNT 1
Expansion: Rib cage expands in forward motion. Note: Breathing remains normal; expansion is not achieved by inhaling but rather by utilizing muscle action.

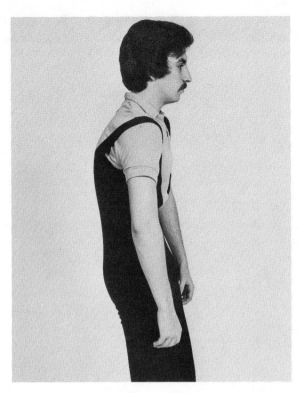

COUNT 2
Contraction: Pull upper torso back as far as possible.

Total rib cage action—side expanding and contracting—also can be done in combination, as: rib cage right, count 1; contract, count 2 (while still holding right); rib cage left, count 3 (while still in contraction); begin to expand, count 4 (rib cage still left). Repeat sequence approximately 4 times and reverse. This exercise also should use a rolling, fluid motion.

HIP ISOLATION

Begin feet and arms in second position, knees flexed (hands could be on hips instead of arms in second).

COUNT 1
Hip moves right. (The accompanying picture may give the illusion of upper torso movement. However, only hip should be moved, weight remaining equally distributed on both feet, knees remaining flexed.)

COUNT 2
Hip returns to center position.

COUNT 3
Hip moves left.

COUNT 4
Hip returns to center position.

This sequence should be repeated for a total of 2-4 times and then done without pausing in the upright position, from 8-16 times.

HIP EXPANSION AND CONTRACTION

Begin as for hip isolation.

*Note: Back stays
in upright position
throughout this
exercise, knees
remaining flexed.*

COUNT 1
Contract hips; hips, buttocks and pelvis pull back.

COUNT 2
Return to upright position.

COUNT 3
Expand hips and pelvis (in forward thrusting motion).

COUNT 4
Return to upright position.

This sequence should be repeated for a total of 2-4 times and then done without pausing in the upright position, from 8-16 times.

KNEE ISOLATION

COUNT 1
Step to right side with right foot (foot and leg turned out), pressing weight to ball of right foot with bent right leg.

COUNT 2
Right knee turns in.

COUNT 3
Return to position used in count 1.

COUNT 4
Right heel drops to floor.

This exercise should be repeated for a total of 4-8 times and then reversed, using other (left) leg.

jazz positions and techniques

This chapter deals with the basic positions of jazz dancing and demonstrates many of the techniques (and, in some cases, it shows the difference between jazz and ballet positions). Combine these positions and techniques with each other—and use them with the stretches and isolations shown in earlier chapters of this book—and you have the basis for choreographing your own jazz-dance sequence. In fact, the following chapter, which demonstrates a jazz-dance combination prepared exclusively for readers of this book, shows exactly how these elements can come together in a lively, flowing dance sequence.

FEET JAZZ 1ST
Stand with feet together, parallel to each other, weight equally distributed, toes pointed forward.

JAZZ HANDS
Fingers and thumb splayed, palms forward. (See also Inverted Jazz Hands, below.)

ARMS 2ND
In 2nd position, arms would be somewhere out to side, i.e., with bent elbows (as illustrated), or extended straight out (below), or diagonal up from elbow or shoulder, or diagonal down from shoulder, etc.

47

JAZZ ARMS EXTENDED 2ND (Palms Down)
(Sometimes also referred to as "long jazz arms.")

INVERTED JAZZ HANDS
Similar to Jazz Hands (above), but palms back, thumbs down.

FEET BALLET 1ST
Heels together, toes turned out to sides. Note: When in this position, try to achieve turn out with entire leg (not just feet), helping to keep excessive weight off inner arch. For jazz look, Arms 2nd and Jazz Hands could be used, as well as other arm positions.

FEET JAZZ 2ND
Feet and legs apart, parallel to each other, toes facing forward.

FEET BALLET 2ND
Feet apart, legs parallel to each other, feet turned out.

FEET JAZZ 4TH
Feet parallel to each other, toes facing forward, legs apart (one leg forward, one leg back).

FEET BALLET 4TH
Legs and feet apart, one leg front, one leg back, as in jazz 4th but with legs and feet utilizing turn out.

FEET BALLET 5TH
One foot (either foot) in front of other, both feet turned out and together (heel of front foot to toe of back foot, heel of back foot to toe of front foot).

FLAT OR TABLE BACK

Feet in Jazz 2nd, legs straight, body bends forward from hip parallel to floor. Note: Arms also may be extended forward, especially if utilizing ballet bar. However, as in most elements of jazz, arm positions are optional.

FOLDED STRETCH POSITION

Legs in Jazz 2nd, hands grasp back of ankles, approaching from outside of legs, upper torso pulled out, head down toward feet. You may approach this Folded Stretch from upright position or by first reaching Flat Back (above), then pulling down on separate counts.

FORWARD TENDU

Standing on one supporting leg, point other leg and foot forward with turn out. Note: Tendu also may be done to side or back.

DEMI-PLIÉ (In 2nd Position)

Demi-plié is a bending of the knees, usually one-half of full bend. In ballet (and to practice a good plié), it is done with derriere tucked in, back straight, head slightly tilted up, feet flat on floor. However, in jazz, there is more license to turn out or in or straight to achieve a look suitable to the choreography. Grand plié in 2nd may be achieved by pressing body closer to floor, body line and feet position remaining same as in demi. Pliés can be done from any position.

GRAND PLIE (In Ballet 1st)
A full bending of the knees, allowing heels to raise as body presses down. To return to standing position, press heels to floor to initiate upward movement. Again, jazz license may be used to allow creative freedom.

DEMI-PLIÉ (In 2nd Position) IN RELEVÉ
Relevé is to raise onto bottoms of toes (demi point). You may achieve this either by a smooth or by a springing motion.

2ND POSITION RELEVÉ, STRAIGHT LEG
Note: You may come to relevé in jazz from any position. In these illustrations of relevé, dancer is utilizing turn out. A combination of pliés and relevés can be achieved by beginning in Jazz or Ballet 2nd position, straight legs, dropping into demi-plié (count 1); spring into relevé—while still in plié (count 2); straighten legs while still in relevé (count 3); drop heels to floor (count 4); and repeat as many times as desired.

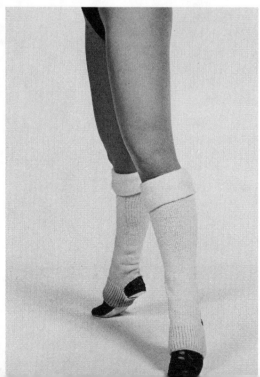

LUNGE FORWARD, FEET JAZZ 4TH
To lunge is to move total upper body over one leg. That leg then becomes the supporting leg and drops into plié during body motion. Note: Lunge can be done in any direction. A forward lunge usually causes a raising to the ball of the back foot.

LUNGE SIDE
Use same technique as Lunge Forward.

This heel pressing technique can be used to exercise the muscles and tendons of the back of the legs, especially the Achilles tendon, and if used as an exercise it should be done a number of times and then reversed to exercise the opposite leg. It also can be done in combination with Grand Battement (description follows).

HEEL PRESS
Begin Forward Lunge with right foot forward, feet in jazz 4th with left foot back on ball. (See above.)

COUNT 1
While keeping weight over supporting leg (right) press left heel to floor.

COUNT AND
Raise left heel off floor.

BATTEMENT FRONT
Raise leg from hip in a low kick (raised foot may be flexed or pointed according to desired effect). Raising leg with flexed foot helps stretch muscles in back of leg.

GRAND BATTEMENT
Raise leg as in Battement but in a higher kick, again with pointed or flexed foot.

Put together a Grand Battement/Heel Press exercise by doing 8 heel presses, then swing back leg to front Grand Battement, count 1; touch back as in starting position of Heel Press, count 2; then do 2 heel presses, counts 3-4. Repeat last 4 counts 4-8 times.

To reverse procedure, from Grand Battement step back left, putting weight on left, step back right on ball of right foot, step in place left with bent left knee. You are now in position to press with right heel.

JAZZ PASSE IN RELEVE
Weight on left foot, left foot high in releve. Raise right knee forward, place arched foot alongside left knee, arm position optional.

BACK ATTITUDE, ARMS 4TH
While standing on one leg, raise other leg from hip with turnout (emphasizing turn out of knee and foot), knee bent, back straight. Again note license taken to achieve jazz look, i.e., supporting leg can be bent or straight, working leg could be with minimum or maximum turn out and raised to any degree, arm position could be as shown in 4th position (one arm forward, one arm over head) with ballet look—or in any other position, done softly (with flowing arms) or strongly (jazz arms and jazz hands).

FRONT ATTITUDE, ARMS MIDDLE 3RD
Stand on one foot while raising other leg forward from hip, knee and foot turned out (as in Back Attitude). Arms may be in Middle 3rd (as shown)—one arm forward and one arm out to side.

BACK ATTITUDE IN RELEVÉ
This illustration depicts Back Attitude (above) in Relevé (high on bottoms of toes), utilizing a chair for home use in place of studio ballet bar to provide balance and some support.

SIDE ATTITUDE
While standing on one leg, raise other leg from hip to side of body with turn out of leg (emphasizing turn out of knee and foot).

PIQUÉ FRONT, ARMS LOW 5TH
While standing on one foot, bend other knee while utilizing turn out in bent leg, placing foot in front of and close to supporting leg between ankle and knee, arched foot utilizing turn out, arms Low 5th.

PIQUÉ BACK
While standing on one foot, other leg utilizes techniques described for Piqué Front, but leg in back.

PIQUÉ BACK IN RELEVÉ
This illustration depicts Piqué Back (above) in Relevé (high on bottoms of toes).

FIRST ARABESQUE
While standing on one foot, raise other leg from hip, straight leg in turn out, foot arched and with turn out. This illustration, depicting one arm diagonal up and one arm diagonal down, shows smooth body line as in ballet. However, keep in mind that jazz license allows variations to achieve a desired look.

PENCHÉ
Stand on one foot, body leaning forward, head down, other foot raised to its highest level with arched foot. Note: This illustration shows penché legs with arched back and head.

SOUS—SUS
Feet in Relevé, legs and feet pulling tightly together (in jazz, with or without turn out), one foot over and one foot under.

HIGH JAZZ WALK (In Relevé)

Note: High jazz walks may be done traveling forward or back with both feet in Relevé, one foot passing the other.

COUNT 1
Both feet in Relevé, left foot steps in front of right, passing thighs, knees and ankles, as stepping Jazz 4th to Jazz 4th in Relevé, arms down, palms down.

COUNT 2
Right foot steps in front of left, still in Relevé, same technique as for count 1.

These High Jazz Walks also may be done in 2nd position: Both feet in Relevé, weight on left foot, body upright over left foot, arms optional 2nd or jazz arms down, count 1; transfer weight from left foot to right foot, still in Relevé, count 2. These walks may be done forward or back with small or Pixie-like steps, legs remaining apart.

"Penguin Look" may be achieved by slight sideward tilt of upper body over supporting leg, with jazz arms down, fingers pointing to sides, palms down.

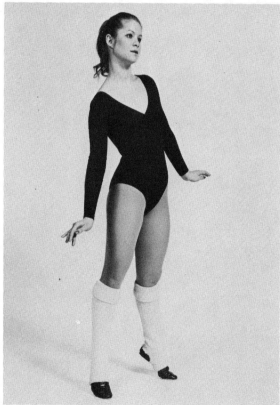

JAZZ WALK FORWARD (Opposition Arms to Legs)

COUNT 1
Feet flat to floor, right foot steps forward with bent right knee, left knee locks, hip over left leg. Right arm pulled back, right shoulder isolation forward, right hand clenched, palm back, left hand up, elbow down, hand clenched, palm forward.

COUNT 2
Left foot steps in front of right, repeating but reversing technique of count 1.

JAZZ RUNS

Begin right foot behind left foot, weight on left foot, both knees bent (in plié), then:

Note: Jazz runs usually are done in a continuous driving motion (no bounce). Legs remain in plié

COUNT 1
Right foot slides on or steps very low to floor with turn out, passing and stepping in front of left in forward lunging motion (left foot utilizing turn out, heel off floor). Right shoulder isolation back, arms optional 2nd and in opposition to feet.

COUNT 2
To continue, reverse foot and body technique.

COMBINATION TOUCH AND SIDE LUNGE

COUNT 1
Both knees bent and close together, weight on left foot, ball of right foot touches floor (no change of weight) close to arch of left foot. left arm forward, right arm side, palms down. Head tilted up. Note: At count 1, head and arms also may be done as in first count of Jazz Combination (see following chapter).

COUNT 2
Right foot and upper torso lunge side, arms raise slightly and pull back, expand rib cage. Note: Count 2 also may be done with lunge forward diagonal.

INSIDE BACK PIQUÉ TURN

Note: Piqué turns for jazz may be done in any number of counts desired to suit choreography. We will show this turn in four illustrations.

NO. 1
Step in Relevé with right foot in front of left, arms and body beginning to turn right.

NO. 2
Left foot raises back of right leg, arms and body continue turning right.

NO. 3
Turn continues.

NO. 4
Piqué turn completed.

Note: Turn may end with foot piqué front and may also be done as outside turn by turning in other direction with same foot. Turn also may, of course, be done using opposite foot.

EXTENDED STAG LEAP

A basic preparation for Extended Stag Leap would be to take a low jump on balls of both feet, both knees bent, arms down. Then spring up one leg extended forward with arched foot, the other back, arms raising to aid leap and to give desired style. Note: Stag leap may be done in a straight up fashion or in a forward motion. In any leap, landing always is made in plié.

STAG LEAP WITH KNEE SCALE

Preparation as in Extended Stag Leap, then: Forward leg bent at knee, both feet arched, arms thrust high over head for lift and look. Second illustration shows beginning of landing.

JAZZ SQUARE

COUNT 1
Right foot crosses front of left.

COUNT 2
Left foot forward front of right.

COUNT 3
Right foot side or back diagonal, hip to right.

COUNT 4
Left foot back or back diagonal, hip left.

Note: Jazz Square may be done leading with either foot.

a special jazz dance combination

In jazz dancing, as in other forms of dance, performance should be the ultimate goal of study and practice. In this chapter, we have choreographed, especially for readers of this book, a jazz-dance combination. It provides a practical demonstration of how many of the basic elements—the jazz-dance positions, the isolations, the movements—that you have learned in the preceding chapters of this book can be structured into one cohesive, flowing dance combination.

Because of the consistent eight-count repetition used throughout this combination, the student will find it adaptable to different types of music. For example, it works well with disco rhythms as well as with a Latin sound and even with swing-type music. As you try matching this combination to music of different rhythms, you will find yourself almost automatically interjecting varying styles of dancing. For example, if you dance this combination to music such as "Rise" by Herb Alpert, you will find it can produce a smooth disco look and feeling.

After you have mastered this combination, try adapting your own variations to it. This way, you can choreograph your own individual jazz-dance combination to fit your particular style and personality. (Note: Unless otherwise indicated, both dancers perform identical movements in the following combination.)

BEGIN
Lunge forward right diagonal, left arm stretching forward, right arm reaching upward forward diagonal, palms down.

COUNT 1
Bring right leg up to jazz passé position, hands clenched into fists, pulling hands in toward chest, elbows up, head down (chin tucked in.)

COUNT 2
Return to beginning position.

COUNT 3
On this count begin back pas de bourrée turn. Left foot crosses back of right, left arm down, entire upper torso pulling left, head looking left, beginning left pivot on ball of left foot.

COUNT AND
Approximately halfway through turn, transfer weight to balls of right foot, continuing pivot. Right hand begins to place at front of right upper hip area, palms in. Left hand begins to place at back of left hip, palms out.

COUNT 4
At completion of turn, cross left foot in front of right, dropping to flat foot in plié left, hands now reaching hip placements. Note: All pivots in this combination are done in relevé.

COUNT 5
Begin jazz square (see chapter on technique), using flexed knees throughout. Right leg crosses in front of left, left arm extended diagonal up (with jazz hands), right arm extended diagonal down (with inverted jazz hands) right shoulder forward isolation.

COUNT 6 (not shown; refer to technique chapter)
Left foot crosses front of right, reversing arms and hands, with left shoulder isolation forward.

COUNT 7 (no shown; refer to technique chapter)
Push off left foot, right foot side or diagonal back, hip pulling right diagonal back, arms and shoulders as in count 5.

COUNT 8 (not shown; refer to technique chapter)
Left foot back or diagonal back, hip and rib cage pulling left, arms and shoulders as in count 6.

Repeat total sequence, but with counts 1-2 lunging directly forward.

COUNT 1
Begin jazz front pas de bourre. Right foot crosses in front of left, legs in demi-plié. Hands tuck in toward chest, palms down, elbows parallel to floor.

COUNT AND
Left leg reaches to side on ball of foot (most of weight remaining on right side of body, although right foot does leave floor at end of this half count). Right arm to side diagonal, palms down, left arm up (bent elbow).

COUNT 2
Weight returns to right foot, heels drop to floor, right leg in plié, right arm diagonal down (palms down), left arm diagonal up (palms down).

Then reverse front jazz pas de bourrée (both arms and feet) on counts 3-AND-4.

Repeat total jazz pas de bourré sequence, counts 1-thru-4, for a total of 8 counts.

COUNT 1
Push off left leg, stepping right foot to right side (feet ballet 2nd), demi-plié. Arms form "W" with head, jazz hands.

COUNT 2
Upper torso moving right (putting weight on right foot), right knee in plié with isolation in, left leg straight. Head turning left over left shoulder, left arm extended to side, hand clenched. Right hand also clenched and placed on right hip, right elbow to right side. (This arm and hand movement often is descriptively called "bow and arrow arms.")

Note: At completion of count 2, begin to transfer upper torso weight to left side of body.

COUNT AND
Left foot to 2nd in relevé. Right arm moves to 2nd position as both arms begin moving upward.

COUNT 3
Right foot steps in place, arms raise into "V," jazz hands. Note: At count 3, legs and arms are straight, (for appearance refer to illustration Count And).

COUNT AND
Upper torso shifts right, placing weight on right foot, right knee bent, isolation in. Right shoulder isolation forward, right hand palm down diagonal back, left arm diagonal up, palm down.

COUNT 4
Touch left in place (no weight change).

COUNT 5
Upper torso twists left, left arm out to side (2nd position) head looking over left arm, right arm swinging in front of body over to left side, right hand clasps left, palm-to-palm, fingers of right hand between fingers and thumb of left (not interlocking). Note: right knee still in isolation.

COUNT 6
Right arm pulls to right, elbow parallel to floor, right hand pulling across chest, left to right (as to draw bowstring), left arm remaining in 2nd, hands clenched. Upper torso still twisted left, head forward.

COUNT 7
In one motion, swivel on balls of both feet, heels moving left, hip moves left, right knee isolation out, head tilts to left side. Left arm to left side, hand clenched, right elbow raises and forearm drives partially across body (fist diagonal down, elbow diagonal up). Left leg remains straight.

COUNT 8
Hip moves from left to right, left knee in plié, isolation out. Swivel on balls of both feet, (heels move from left to right) right leg straight. Head moves from left side tilt to right side tilt, left arm extended to side, hand clenched, right elbow swings upward, around and down in circular motion (elbow down, fist up).

COUNT 1
Push off left foot to right, upper torso over right leg, arms sweep upward into "V" position.

COUNT 2
Left foot crosses back of right (touch only; do not place weight on left foot), arms, led by fingers, make outward circle down. Left shoulder isolation forward.

COUNTS 3-4 (not illustrated)
Reverse side cross, pushing off right, stepping side left, crossing right foot behind left (touch only; do not place weight on right foot). Note: Arms continue to move downward from counts 1-2. Then bring hands up in front of and close to body, hands close together. As hands approach chin they separate and continue up to "V" position over head, palms turning out, reaching "V" position at count 3, left foot side. Arms continue down, palms down, ending as in previous illustration (count 2) on count 4, right leg touching back of left.

COUNT 5
Grand battement with right leg, foot arched, left arm diagonal up, palms forward, right arm rounded 2nd.

COUNT 6
Right leg pulls down and touches back, upper torso twisting to left, right arm stretching forward.

COUNT 7
Begin outside turn, pivoting on ball of left foot, body turning right, right foot in jazz piqué or passé position. Hands approaching front hip area, palms in, jazz hands.

COUNT 8
Complete turn, hands now on front of hips. (This turn could extend beyond full revolution, ending diagonal right.) Note: Two counts have been allotted to this turn to allow double or triple pivots for more advanced dancers.

COUNT 1
Make a very low jump, feet together, and in plié both feet, elbows pulled into sides, forearms extended foward, hands clenched, head slightly down.

COUNT AND
This illustration shows two forms of stag leap, Lisa doing extended stag leap, Mark doing stag leap with knee scale (note arched feet). Right arm extended diagonal up, palms down, left arm forward, palms down. Head turning left, looking over left arm.

COUNT 2
Land on right foot, continue dropping as right leg goes into plié. Left foot touch back with flexed knee and turned out foot.

COUNT 3
Begin triplet. Step forward left in relevé, arms 2nd.

COUNT AND (not illustrated)
Step forward right in relevé (both feet now in relevé). Arms continue upward, index fingers approaching each other, palms forward. Then hands begin to tilt down (as though to dive).

COUNT 4
Left foot forward and crossing in front of right, dropping to left heel into plié. Hands drive down alongside or in front of thighs, inverted jazz hands, head down.

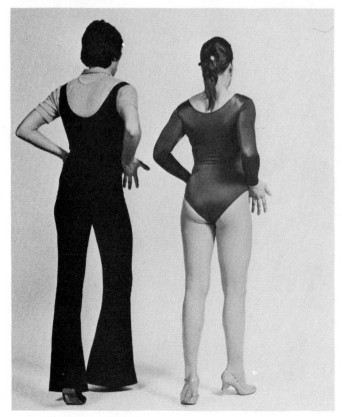

COUNT 5
Feet in relevé, pivoting on both feet, right shoulder back, elbows and hands pulling up to approximately waist height, turning jazz hands (palms out).

COUNT 6
Continue until full turn is executed, dropping on right heel, still on ball of left foot, legs in plié, jazz hand and arms down.

COUNT 7
Jump on both feet, arms pulling up to 2nd, palms down.

COUNT AND
Hop on right leg, right knee beginning to bend, left leg extended back (still elevated), arms pulling up over head to approximate "V" position (palms in, elbows bent).

COUNT 8
Right leg continues to bend (in plié) allowing extended left foot to touch floor with entire inside of foot (foot in turn out, heel dropped to floor). Right arm extended side diagonal up, left arm extended forward, palms down.

COUNT 1
Left foot crosses back of right (touch floor but do not transfer weight), right jazz hand, palm in on right hip, left arm diagonal up, jazz hand. Head forward.

COUNT 2
Left foot steps side, ballet or jazz 2nd. Both hands on front of hips, elbows pulling slightly forward, head forward and down. Slight isolation forward both shoulders and slight rib cage contraction.

COUNT 3
Right foot crosses back of left to touch floor, release rib cage contraction. Left hand remains on front of hip, right arm diagonal up, jazz hand, head looking toward jazz hand.

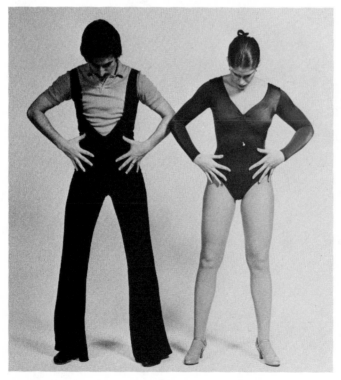

COUNT 4
Right foot step side (ballet or jazz 2nd), both hands in front of hips, head down, shoulder isolation forward, slight contraction of rib cage.

COUNT 5
Repeat movement of count 1, this sequence.

COUNT 6
Repeat movement of count 2, this sequence.

COUNT 7
Raise on ball of right foot, right knee isolation in, lock left leg, hip to left, rib cage pulls to right, right arm extended slight diagonal down, left arm extended diagonal up, hands clenched, palms down, hips pulling to left.

COUNT 8
Shift weight to ball of left foot, left knee plié forward or isolation in. hips move to right side, rib cage pulls left. Right arm remains diagonal down, left arm remains diagonal up.

COUNT 1
Begin back jazz pas de bourrée, right foot crosses back of left on ball of right foot (both knees slightly bent), elbows up parallel to floor, hands clenched and pulling toward chest, head forward and down.

COUNT AND
Left leg extends to left side on ball of left foot. (Although right foot will step on next count, very little weight is put on left.) Head upright, arms begin moving away from body for next count, rib cage beginning to pull right.

COUNT 2
Weight returns to right foot (right foot flat on floor), rib cage pulls right. Right arm to side diagonal down, palm down, left arm to side, slight diagonal forward and up, palm down, right shoulder isolation forward, right knee in plié. Head facing forward or slightly to left.

COUNT 3-AND-4
Reverse count 1-AND-2 (executing back pas de bourrée with left foot).

COUNT 5
Begin fan turn, weight over left foot, body begins to turn right, head looks over right shoulder, right arm begins to pull back, both elbows up, inverted jazz hands, left hand approaches front of left hip, left knee bent, right leg begins to swing back.

COUNT 6
To complete last half of turn, bend right knee, right foot off floor, right foot front piqué, then right foot crosses front of left. Upper torso (including head) tilts side right. Right arm extended to side, jazz hand, palm of left hand on left hip.

COUNT 7
Step side right on ball of right foot, right knee isolation in, left foot flat to floor, left leg locked, hip to left, head tilt to left side, right shoulder isolation forward. Right arm pulling back with bent elbow, palm back, hand clenched, left arm side diagonal up, elbow slightly bent, palm forward, hand clenched.

COUNT 8
Hip shifts to right side, right heel drops to floor (flat foot), up on ball of left foot, left knee isolation in, right leg locked, left shoulder isolation forward. Left arm pulls back, elbow bent, palm back, hand clenched. Right arm side diagonal up, slightly bent elbow, palm forward, hand clenched. Head tilt right.

Total combination should be repeated in reverse for equal emphasis on other side of body. (People have a tendency to dance to their dominant side—right or left—and this will help to develop dexterity.)

index